Minter-isms

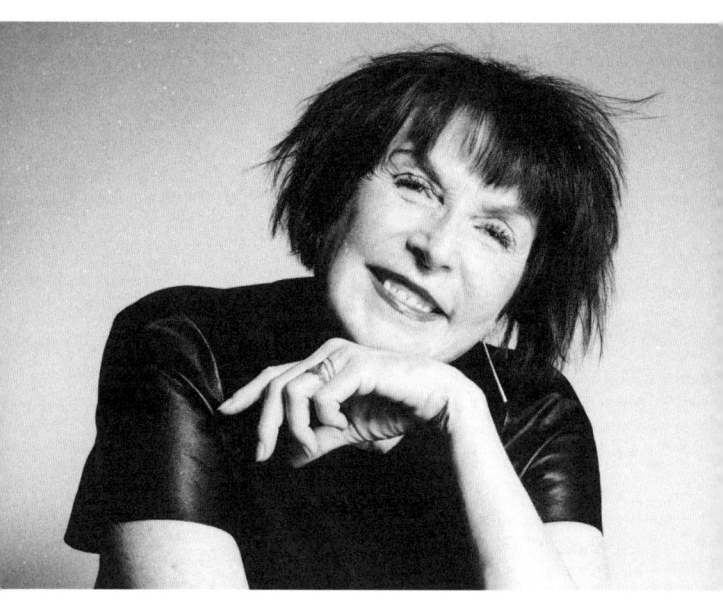

Minter-isms

Marilyn Minter

Edited by Larry Warsh

PRINCETON UNIVERSITY PRESS
Princeton and Oxford

in association with
No More Rulers

Princeton University Press is committed to the protection of
copyright and the intellectual property our authors entrust to us.
Copyright promotes the progress and integrity of knowledge created
by humans. Thank you for supporting free speech and the global
exchange of ideas by purchasing an authorized edition of this
book. If you wish to reproduce or distribute any part of it in
any form, please obtain permission.

Requests for permission to reproduce material from this work
should be sent to permissions@press.princeton.edu

Published by Princeton University Press, 41
William Street, Princeton, New Jersey 08540

In the United Kingdom: Princeton University Press,
99 Banbury Road, Oxford OX2 6JX
press.princeton.edu
in association with
No More Rulers
nomorerulers.com
ISMs is a trademark of No More Rulers, Inc.

ℙ PRINCETON   ~~NO MORE RULERS~~ ®

All Rights Reserved
ISBN 9780691271569

Library of Congress Control Number: 2024944424
British Library Cataloging-in-Publication Data is available

This book has been composed in Johanna MT
Printed in China
1 3 5 7 9 10 8 6 4 2

CONTENTS

INTRODUCTION

Marilyn Minter is the definition of a contemporary woman artist. She is dynamic, ambitious, proactive, playful, and tenacious. Above all, she is authentic. She proclaims the female body and the realms of female sensuality in bright, bold artworks that embody her profound appreciation of women's pleasure and power. When she speaks of these aspects of her work, her lively sense of humor infuses her words with a buoyant charm that belies her status as a distinguished creative figure of her generation.

Marilyn understands the power of her images, and how these images push forward the conversations around sex, sexism, women, and representation in a contemporary world that is obsessed with women's bodies. She understands women and their pleasure. She understands seduction as an imaginative possibility to be explored in the realms of artmaking. And she understands how to put women first when it comes to art history.

Back in the 1980s, I knew of Marilyn by way of our shared orbit around local—soon to be global—legends like Keith Haring and Jean-Michel Basquiat, and the quicksilver cast of characters who defined the ethos of the downtown art scene. Marilyn worked extremely hard during those years as she built her creative career and found personal harmony in what was, for many, an era of wild and risky distractions.

The expanse of Marilyn's art practice—over five decades and counting—reveals a determination to define a painterly language on her own terms. She has always fought for equality, reclaiming images of women for women. Yet that came at a price. At one time Marylin's work was discredited for its emphatic sexual content. The critics have always been hard on female artists, and they were especially harsh toward Marilyn for her use of pornography and other sexual imagery at a time when few artists were working with this content.

Fast-forward to the present moment. We cannot ignore the proliferation of overt sexual imagery—and the success of the porn industry—as an aspect of global visual culture. One could say, in fact, that the contemporary world is saturated with sex as a mode of expression and control. Through her reexamination of pornography, and by promoting it as a legitimate category within visual-arts aesthetics, Marilyn can be understood as a pioneer of a "sex-positive" art movement. Her recontextualization of pornography was well ahead of the curve, and time has proven the significance of her artistic choices. She has effectively invented her own visual language for sex in art.

The scale of Marilyn's work emphasizes the sheer physicality of the female body in no uncertain terms. With today's expanded vocabulary for discussing the complexities of sex and sexual identity, we can appreciate Marilyn's use of sexual imagery and female bodies in a much wider cultural context. We might even consider her early pornographic art to be an extension of the classic still life, in which the stationary object—in her case, the human body—is gloried for its simple ontology. Marilyn takes the sensual aspects of pornography and connects them to art history: fluids as paint, and as an essential part of our corporeal nature.

Most recently, Marilyn has embraced new technologies to create stunning images in an innovative and original process that combines her mastery of photography and painting with cutting-edge digital tools. Starting from photographic source material, she layers, enhances, and empowers it to yield a new medium with its own look and impact. Brush, camera, and pixels—the traditional and the digital—are her creative materials.

Marilyn's collaborations with leading female cultural figures—including Madonna, Lady Gaga, Lizzo, and other women of our time—have carried her art to a global audience. Other projects affirm her interest in the fashion, advertising, and cosmetics industries and their role in shaping our ideas of beauty and worth. Imperfection is a vital part of her art. She champions sweat, freckles, body hair, and signs of age, all of which are usually removed from images in the media. Emerging in her work, these dynamics create distinct metaphors and paradoxes, as intriguing as they are visually sumptuous. Imperfection is Marilyn's perfection.

In recent years, it has been a delight getting to know Marilyn more closely while working with her on a number of curated projects, including this book. Our diverse conversations became the basis for this volume, and it is an honor to share her voice in these pages. Marilyn's bedrock beliefs as an artist and feminist come through in every word, revealing her wit and wisecrack spirit. Her rebellious energy is inspiring a new epoch of badass female artists. Marilyn is a cultural icon of our time—the ultimate "bad girl," in the best way.

LARRY WARSH
NEW YORK CITY
JANUARY 2024

Minter-isms

Early Years

I started making art practically as soon
as I could walk. (46)

———

I started painting when I was about 12 years
old. Terrible self-taught paintings about social
issues. When I was a freshman in college I
had to take a painting class. (44)

———

When I was 13, I started drinking. The first
time I got high, I said to myself, "Oh, this
is what normal feels like." (24)

———

I grew up with my dad dating girls that were
18 when I was 16. There's this old man, and
then these really beautiful young girls.
It was very distorting. (48)

I was always really rebellious. I was put in jail
at 16! I changed people's driver's licenses, so
they could go to the bars and buy booze. (28)

I got my license taken away three times
before I was 21. (37)

I was a bad kid because I had a drug addict mother, but I was the worst kind of kid you could have if you were a drug addict, because I was uncontrollable. I would stay out all night and make her frantic. (37)

———

When everybody else was into Haight-Ashbury and getting stoned, I did speed and listened to the Velvet Underground and wanted to come to NYC. (44)

———

I used to think I was the worst person that ever lived, and that's pretty narcissistic of me. I wasn't even close. (37)

———

I remember when I was a little girl and the World War II generation was complaining that TV was warping the youth. But I think television was just information, and I think it made my age-group into these '60s revolutionaries—we had access to so much more information. We made our own decisions about race and politics instead of taking everything for granted. (27)

———

I went to a school at University of Florida; it was very conservative. And if you weren't an Abstract Expressionist you were considered not a true artist, not a real artist, you didn't count. (42)

———

I knew I was going to be an artist, I just didn't know what kind. (45)

———

My whole life was about trying to get to New York City so I could go to the Factory and meet Andy Warhol. (5)

———

When I was an undergraduate, I called the Factory to learn how to make silk screens, and they told me. (6)

———

I got a C in painting, and I got an A in photography, so I decided to major in photography. (6)

———

I knew I wanted to go where Warhol was. I'd
never been up north. I'd never even seen snow.
I was too scared to go straight to NYC even
though I got into Pratt. I also got into Syracuse
with a scholarship and that was close enough
for me. I went from never seeing snow
to 156 inches the first year. (44)

In art school I was the only female, there were
17 guys, and most of them knew how to work
in the woodshop. I really didn't, and I think
that put me at a real disadvantage. So I learned
right away how to use the equipment, and
that got me a little respect. (37)

I come from severe dysfunction, and that's why I'm an artist. (32)

———

I started drawing at five years old. I started working with glamour. (6)

———

Then I won this award from the Everson Museum; for my very first semester there I won the painting award where they bought the piece. So that made the faculty pay attention to me. (37)

———

I took those photos of my mother in 1969 when I was in undergrad. People thought they were shocking, and I felt waves of shame after I showed them to my classmates. My mom was a drug addict living down in Florida, and just such a mess. (22)

———

I wasn't taking photos of my mother to romanticize the horrors of her shut-in life, but that's how they were interpreted. (25)

———

I moved to New York in 1976 after grad school at Syracuse University. The years that followed were exciting and productive, but in 1985, I entered rehab. (24)

———

I came to the city and went wild! I divorced my husband. And got into drugs and alcohol, and partied real hard. Anyway, I basically ended up in both in- and outpatient rehab, and I got clean and sober. (44)

———

Everyone would come into my studio and say, "you gotta loosen up." And so I thought, well, if I got high enough I would loosen up, because I had no faith in myself. (40)

———

[When I first moved to New York] I did meet artists because I worked as a plumber's assistant. (20)

I love teaching, and that is how I have
survived in New York City. (54)

———

I cobbled together all these jobs. I was
teaching art at night to retired people in
Brooklyn. Because I could copy anything, I did
gigs at the Met, and I'd be on display copying
stuff when they brought tours around. (46)

———

I listened to other people more than my
inner voice when I was younger. If I had to do
it over, I would only listen to that inner voice.
It's a lesson I have to learn over and over. (49)

———

I don't say, "Oh, gee, back in the day."
I find that very defeating. Back in the day
for me is right now. I love today. (47)

———

People love my early work now. At the time,
nobody could see it. I'm glad I didn't destroy
that. And it gave me street cred. I lived
through being eviscerated by the art world.
What doesn't kill you makes you
stronger, right? (4)

———

Art and Sexuality

Sex is the most powerful instinct
in the universe. (35)

———

I'm interested in art that's about the times
we live in, and pornography is part of that.
I started looking at the way we present
ourselves in the culture as female. (12)

———

I thought if women worked with porn, they
were soft-core. I just thought, "I'll see what
happens if I do hard-core." (4)

———

My whole goal was to see if it would change
the meaning if women owned sexual imagery,
if we actually started making imagery for
our own pleasure and amusement. (7)

———

It struck me that, from the beginning of
art history, almost all paintings of women
grooming [themselves] have been made by
men. I wanted to know whether it would
change the meaning if, as a woman,
I painted other women bathing. (1)

———

Everything I make is gorgeous, to suck you in and seduce you, and that includes a lot of things that don't fit the established beauty ideals. (22)

———

My work is really about seducing you with craft. (34)

———

Every single picture you see pretty much taken from advertising is sexual content—sex sells! So it's not like I have to go very far. And so, I am just using what's available, talking about the culture that we live in. Sex rules. (31)

———

Pornography is one of those giant industries of culture, even though many people have so much contempt for it and consider it shallow and superficial. But actually, there would be no internet without pornography. ... [I]t doesn't make sense that artists are ignoring this huge billion-dollar industry. (12)

Why would we dismiss glamour and fashion when they are giant cultural engines? Why would we dismiss pornography as shallow and debased? (8)

Everyone loves their children and porn. (10)

———

I'm a sexual creature. People always ask me about my sex life, and I think I have a healthy one, but I don't think it's abnormal. Nobody has politically correct fantasies, and I don't have any shame about that. (32)

———

I can paint spit strands but if I paint it so beautifully then it's not going to make you want to gag. (23)

———

When I was making my first statement about sexual imagery, there was only a handful of people doing this. It was this nascent group of pro-sex feminists, mostly lesbians, they were my support system. (7)

———

In [Cindy Sherman's] work, sex was demonized, and mine was about pleasure. So she was embraced. I didn't know she was doing it. I got compared to her, which was my worst nightmare, because she was my idol. (44)

———

When it comes to sexual imagery even the most enlightened people can become paralyzed. (44)

———

All the images that I chose were images that I found compelling or somewhat funny. I wasn't thinking in terms of trying to turn you on, I was trying to see if it changes the meaning if women make sexual imagery. (13)

———

Sexuality is so loaded and whenever anyone
tries to define it, it will just bite you in the
butt ... somebody's fetish will be your disgust.
(35)

I can only find about fifteen paintings that
have pubic hair in art history, in all the
millions of paintings that have been made. ...
Pubic hair hardly exists in art history.
It was considered vulgar. (12)

You never see a bush in art history. Why is
that? It's not an ugly thing. (38)

Nobody writes about wrinkles or pubic hair.
And the pubic hair, I never tried to make
sexual. I just tried to make it beautiful. (40)

———

Men find it threatening when young, beautiful
girls make sexual imagery, but if you're an
old lady like me, then you can do
anything you want. (1)

———

What I am always trying to do is make a
picture of what it feels like to look, and there
are levels of emotions that go on when
you see a glamorous image. (40)

———

I support any woman using sexual imagery,
and I try to give a picture of what it's like to
identify as female, what it feels like to be
constantly looked at. (1)

———

That's where the female gaze comes
in too. The Lisa Taddeos and Sally Rooneys
and Jennifer Egans—they have such a
fresh way of looking at sex. I'm so
impressed by them. (19)

———

There were earlier female artists dealing with sexuality, like Lynda Benglis, Carolee Schneemann, Judy Bernstein, and Joan Semmel, and I recently found out about the wonderful Betty Tompkins, who was actually way more graphic than all of us! It was a very small group. Lynda, Carolee, and I were in shows together during this time. We were a small group of pro-sex feminist artists—it was a nascent movement. (44)

———

And then that one photo of Lynda Benglis in *Artforum*, which I thought was brilliant. (42)

———

There is always resistance to sexual imagery if
women are the agency. Women are supposed
to be the objects of sexual desire and when
women own the agency of it or production
of it, it becomes a lot of trouble. (2)

———

I had a good career start, but it all stopped
when I did hard-core porn work. (13)

———

I was raising questions about the authorship
of porn. I was taking imagery from an abusive
history and repurposing it. It was at the height
of political correctness and most feminists
that didn't think like that yet. (12)

———

Feminists of my age were horrified by women owning their sexuality. I was ahead of my time. I thought that everyone shared my opinion because I was in a group of pro-sex feminists. I was attending National Organization for Women meetings and defending abortion clinics, so to be called a traitor to feminism was a real shock. (1)

———

This level of feminism coming out of the 1970s was really anti-men and anti-sex. Taking porn and owning it for your own amusement and pleasure, as I did, was seen as a slap in the face. I got where the fear came from, but there was a group of feminists who were trying to ban sexual imagery, and I was the antithesis of that. (1)

———

I was accused of being complicit in sexism and was stunned by the idea that a woman owning sexual imagery could be taken so negatively. For me it was a way of empowering myself. (5)

———

That was one of the reasons people were so angry at me: they didn't want to be called prudes so they said the work was boring. They were really offended by the fact that women would even make sexual imagery. (12)

———

There is no universal anything when it comes to sexuality. I find if you try and put everyone and everything into categories and you think everything is black and white, nothing is black and white. Maybe death. And the sun rising.

(53)

———

Yesterday's smut is today's erotica. (13)

———

Making Art: Inspiration and Techniques

As artists, our jobs are to take pictures of the way we live, to make images out of chaos that talk about who we are today. (19)

———

I am an image maker, and I am a trickster. (2)

———

I am interested in making pictures of things you haven't seen before, even though we know they are there. (7)

———

My interest in beauty and fashion has more to do with emphasizing what's there but hasn't been photographed before or gets airbrushed out, like the lines on your legs when you pull your socks down, the dirt, sweat, armpit hair, pimples, and freckles. (22)

─────

The whole beauty industry is all-encompassing. Glamour, fashion, and porn, for that matter, are giant engines of the culture. They are also considered contemptible, dismissible, and superficial, but they also give people so much pleasure. I like to pick that binary apart in my work. (23)

─────

There has been so much nuance, and that is where my work has always been—in the nuance, in the gray areas. I am often sidelined for not being critical, but that's not my job. My job is to make a picture—to have both points of view in the same image, and you come to your own conclusions. (8)

———

I like to work with humor much more than anger. It's not that I am not angry, but I think humor is so much more powerful. (7)

I know there is always going to be suspicion of anything that's too seductive, but I like the idea of making paradoxes in everything I do. I want there to be multiple layers and to have anything that might be disturbing. I want to create such a beautiful soup that you can actually be able to see another layer because I make it look so good, or I try to anyway. (23)

I could work for 18 hours on a drawing. I got total pleasure out of it. (42)

The only difference really, between what I am doing and advertising is [that] they have a product to sell, and if I am selling anything, it's a vision of what goes wrong. (17)

I can work on four or five paintings at a time, because I have assistants. Every square inch of a painting gets special attention. I tell people what to do, or I do it, until I get the image that I know I want. (12)

———

I have always been interested in doing billboards. Ideally, it is going to just stop you for a second, just to think about what it means. If it comes across as slightly subversive as an intervention, that's okay too.
I am selling my truth. (16)

———

[Earlier in my career] I was making cum-shot paintings. At that point in time, there was no internet. To get source images, I had to go to all these hard-core porn stores on 42nd Street and Wall Street. I would walk down the aisle and it would clear! They must have thought I was an aging porn star. I didn't think I was doing anything shocking. I was just making my art from my own vision. (1)

———

I love learning from the professionals, whether it's about lighting or doing hair. I never knew anything about fashion or beauty before. (4)

———

Working with the beauty industry, which includes fashion, models, accessories, and makeup, gave me so many ideas for paintings. I did projects for M·A·C Cosmetics, Tom Ford, and Jimmy Choo, and made whole bodies of work from the outtakes of those commercial shoots. (22)

———

Whenever I take on a commercial job, I'm always piggybacking. I don't take on a job unless they give me a lot of freedom. (4)

———

I have always been interested in people with so-called flaws. ... The models start to sweat under the lights, it's a real thing. Peoples' feet do get dirty, even if they are in very expensive shoes. No one really makes an image of that. (16)

———

Nothing leaves [my studio] unless I am in love with it. (23)

———

You have to act yourself into right thinking. You can't sit there and smoke cigarettes and look at the wall waiting for inspiration. (9)

———

When I'm stuck I just keep working and make terrible-looking things until something else comes out of it. That's the creative process. Work comes from work. (9)

———

I am not afraid of technology. I like playing with it, I like finding things. I love exploring. I am really a very curious person. (7)

———

I am more concerned with creating depth and translucency via layering with enamel paint (very thin layers are not opaque) rather than trying to make something look super realistic. (39)

———

I like working with digital media. Going from analogue to digital, you lose something but simultaneously gain something extraordinary that at this point has no limits. I have years of painting experience that I am expanding through all these new tools. I am very enthusiastic about the new slow-motion video cameras like the Phantom 4K. I like slowing things down so much that new meanings develop. I am not afraid of change. (39)

———

There was this long period of time when I was making terrible things, because I was trying to be an Expressionist painter. I wanted to fit into the dialogue, but it looked phony. (46)

———

[I describe myself as a sculptor.] I've always
thought of it that way. I'm building
this surface and it's just really thin,
but it's sculpture. (4)

———

I started experimenting with dripping, and
the drip paintings ended up as *Food Porn*. I let
the paintings drip and then hand-painted the
dot screens. It's fake mechanization.
Fake Expressionism. (46)

———

The way I start my process is first take a
photograph, print it out, and I make a
decision which ones turn into photographs
and which ones turn into paintings. But once
in a while, I know when an image will
be a perfect painting. (16)

———

I work with enamel paint; it's layers and
layers of enamel on metal, and that's why
my paintings look slightly different than
oil paintings. (16)

———

Once I saw Photoshop, that was it—I thought
I had died and went to heaven. I stopped
drawing! I did all my drawing on Photoshop.
(27)

———

I could do one show a year and I still didn't have enough paintings, so I'd have to put the photos in to fill up the space. The photos for me are like drawings for a traditional artist. Now, the paintings are totally done in Photoshop, take about a week to do, to put together each one. (4)

———

Once I learned how to make something from a photograph, I learned how to make my paintings. (12)

———

The thrill of photorealism is that when the viewer gets close to the painting it looks just like a photo. But if you get close to my paintings they just fall apart; the closer you get, the more abstract it gets. (12)

———

With the photorealists you can go right up to it with a magnifying glass, and they are perfect. So I say, well, I am not really copying, I am replacing. I like the idea of replacing the photograph with this paint. I have coined a phrase, I am a photo-replacer. (31)

———

When people say to me: "Oh, you are painting from a photo," that's actually not true. I am painting from an actual creation of a reference and I change it constantly. (15)

Anything that you see that's painted is a construct. It never existed as a photo. (23)

The photos are just these beautiful, perfect photos. The paintings are like Frankenstein. I used the necklace from one negative, and the lips from another, and a drip from another. None of that exists as a photo. (56)

Once I make the reference, I can start a painting. I start with that as the "bones of the painting" and then it morphs, it changes, they get smarter as I work on them. The paintings teach me what I'm going to do and what I'm going to make with the next one. (12)

———

Enamel paintings take about a year or over a year to make, especially the large ones. If you look at the paintings and you look at the photographs in the same room, you will see there is a huge difference. There is a depth and richness in the paintings that you could never get in a photo. (15)

———

I probably would have been okay with just painting in the studio by myself forever but fuck it. I wanted to take photos and make videos, and I think it's made me a better artist; the experiences expanded the scope of my work and how I think. (30)

———

About 2009 I started working behind glass, because so much imagery that we see is behind glass, and I just thought that that's how we perceive advertising, it's almost always protected. ... I don't really think it's interesting to make another pretty face or another good-looking ad. I just want to make a picture of what it's like to live in a world where you are constantly bombarded with images and they are not necessarily precious anymore. (15)

———

I am using glass in front of everything.
The water, the wetness, the dripping is
another barrier to just dampen the narrative
so I am not telling you what to think. (40)

———

I work with steam, you never know what
it's going to do. So you just have to be willing
to go there at that moment. (55)

———

Steam disappears fast, so I actually use
frozen glass and it creates the illusion
of steam. (43)

This liquid that I use all the time, it's candy and vodka mixed together. (42)

———

I shoot a lot of video these days. ... I'm shooting behind glass a lot. It's sort of getting more and more abstract. ... I'm sort of allergic to narrative. (42)

———

I learned all kinds of photography techniques because I worked with commercial photographers and commercial lighting directors. (38)

———

When I'm making my art, I don't ever use makeup artists. I just don't want to disappoint them. I like it when the models start to sweat, when people get wet and glistening. (28)

———

My work is all about contradictions
and paradox. (35)

———

I am trying to zone-in on the overlooked. (40)

———

Women and Power

There's this constant distortion that's happening between all of us—men and women—there's a sense of failure. But at the same time, all of this pleasure. (29)

———

I have always worked with things that are considered contemptible. I was taking abusive imagery and repurposing it. A lot of feminists in my generation were coming from fear and here I was taking power and trying to own it.
(38)

———

It's a real taboo for women to own sexual power and it's amazing to me that more artists aren't examining this. (33)

———

I own sexual agency every chance I get. (40)

———

That's the most powerful thing in the world—
owning your own sexuality. That seems to
frighten a lot of people, and I don't
understand why. I think it is healthier
for everybody. (27)

———

We're never going to get rid of sexual imagery.
Sex rules the world. But women can be the
agents and producers of it. I think it'll be
healthier. All we are asking is to share power.
We're not trying to take over. (19)

———

Women being the agents of their own sexuality is surprising to the world, especially if you're young. I see young women artists working with sexuality and they just get slut-shamed all over the place. It's really upsetting to me. If there's any way to destroy some young, beautiful woman, they're gonna find it. (32)

———

This is a real glass ceiling and I see it all the time, where both men and women go crazy when young women work with sexual imagery. (42)

———

Look at how people hate on Tracey Emin, or hate on Laurel Nakadate. Women just aren't allowed by our culture to use sexual imagery in their art until they are old ladies! (44)

———

There's a famous photograph that Robert Mapplethorpe took of Louise Bourgeois holding what looks like a giant dildo [*Louise Bourgeois with Fillette* (1968), 1982] and everyone thinks it's adorable, but if she were a young woman then people would be horrified— other women would be attacking her. (1)

———

And look at Alice Neel. My god, she was totally ignored! (1)

———

I'm really glad to see mediocre women artists getting lots of attention, because the boys have been doing it for years. It's about time we're allowed mediocre women, too. (4)

───────

I want to empower women to stick together more. Boy artists stick together and help each other get to the top. I want women to start acting as a team. I decided in the '90s that I would start saying, "I don't care who it is, but I won't be the only woman in this show." (8)

───────

I would like artists to support other artists. I would like women collectors to start stepping the fuck up, and I'd like all women artists to support other women artists. Work as a team, the boys are able to do that. (35)

———

I've always gravitated toward women like Madonna and Pamela Anderson—they make a lot of money because they own their own agency. Pamela Anderson is a pinup; that's how she makes her money. But she's not an Anna Nicole Smith or Marilyn Monroe, someone constantly being the victim of some Svengalis. They are using everything they've got to earn a living. Why not? (27)

———

We're relooking at how we treated Monica Lewinsky and Britney Spears. We're appalled at the way we behaved toward these young women. (19)

———

I think women really believe that the patriarchy will take care of them. They really want that strong presence—somebody who will let them nest. It may be cultural, or it may be intuitive. But what I know from life is that nobody can take care of anybody. You have to take care of yourself. (8)

———

You get cherished and treated well when you do estimable things, not when you're a doormat. (8)

———

The shaming of people I find really horrifying. Shame is causing so much pain in this world for no reason. Guilt is fine ... I think guilt is a healthy thing. You can change your behaviors if you are guilty, you can make amends. But shame, your very existence means you are wrong, you are bad, you shouldn't be part of humanity—and that is what we are doing constantly, is shaming women: slut-shaming women, shaming men and women for having unconventional desires. What is so great about conventional desires? Why is that privileged? (7)

Look at what happens to trans people, people born in the wrong body. Secrets will distort you. If you talk about it, you can find health and self-love instead of feeling like the monster from hell or whatever the monster is. (37)

———

My generation of men rarely had powerful women in their lives. The women were mothers, nurses, stewardesses, teachers, etc. Those are important vocations, of course, but there were no female doctors, scientists, lawyers, or heads of universities. Younger generations are more used to women in power and are therefore more comfortable with it. My generation just didn't perceive women that way, which made it that much harder for women to break through. (18)

———

Millennials are so much better than my age-group, you know? They sort of stick together and I love that. They are really supporting one another as women and calling out things like slut-shaming. It's a new phenomenon. (27)

———

[Regarding the series *We Fight to Build a Free World*] It's trying to reclaim the word. The idea [is] that if we're going to be called cunts, I'm going to shove it down your throat. I took it from queer theory, the idea of owning and reclaiming, and did a whole series called *My Cuntry 'Tis of Thee*. It's friends and collaborators, writing on steam, on glass, with phrases like "No Cuntry for Old Men" or "Cuntroversy."

(25)

———

I still don't have an answer to the question, "Did it change the meaning if a woman made these things?" I was just trying to ask questions. I think if you ask questions, people expect you to have answers. Well, I didn't have any answers. I think that was maybe why I was so badly criticized. (12)

I still really wanted to make a case for bringing pubic hair back, so I decided to make a whole series of paintings that would be beautiful enough to put in your living room. (1)

I am interested in the things that the culture called "debased" or "low" culture, because I think it's a lot more powerful than received ideas of what is important. (40)

———

I've always been slightly marginalized, which I don't mind. (44)

———

With my generation, we got birth control for the first time and we went wild. We tried to be like the boys. (32)

The prejudices against women, porn, and fashion have all evolved. Life is more nuanced, and binaries are less popular. People are questioning their knee-jerk reactions. (49)

———

You can be a feminist and be a housewife. You can be a sexual being and be a feminist. (28)

———

I won't be the only woman in a show. I just won't do it. When a show is curated, it has to have other women in, too. (27)

———

I'm still one of the old ladies that doesn't make the money that the boys make that are in my age-group, but that's OK, I'm not complaining. (32)

———

We are so programmed to fight each other. I'm always telling young girls to stick together. (29)

———

Once you're past menopause, people just think you're cute. (8)

The world loves young bad boys and old ladies. Sometimes they love "bad girls" but then only if you can sustain it. Those are the ones I emulate. (11)

———

When you're postmenopausal, you can do anything. You're just adorable. It's pretty shocking, actually. (27)

———

Women need to own production, to be the producers of our own images for our own amusement and pleasure. We need more pictures of who we are. (19)

———

Art and Activism

Artists are empathetic. You can always count on artists to make something that is poignant. They are deeply touched by injustice. They are interpreters of the times we live in, and you can count on them. There might be some that aren't, but I've never met one! (25)

———

I think most people actually can't bear to look at injustice. There is always something one can do and that's what I learned early on. And especially now, we just can't afford to be silent. I feel like democracy is just hanging by a thread. (2)

———

I think that if you're not angry and upset, you're not paying attention right now. (14)

———

I always wondered: "During the fascism of the early 20th century—how could people support it?" And now I see it's a fear of losing something you never had to begin with. I'm hoping we can keep it from happening this time because we have so much more information. (25)

———

We're fighting fascism now in the United States. I've never seen democracy so fragile— and I'm old. I saw Nixon, I saw the AIDS crisis, I saw Reagan, and this is the worst it's ever been. (33)

———

Weimar Germany didn't have the internet. The difference is that we can stop another Crystal Night before it happens. (8)

―――

I hate sexism. I hate racism. I hate homophobia. And I hate political correctness. I hate all of those things. (44)

―――

I don't know if my art has made any difference anywhere but in the art world, but my activism has raised money for progressive causes. (3)

―――

I'm not much of a philosopher but I'm good at coming up with ideas to raise money for causes I feel strongly about. (12)

———

I have always been an activist ever since I can remember. I am not really an activist-artist, that's Barbara Kruger who is a genius at it. I just happen to be a painter and an artist who happens to be an activist; they have always run parallel in my life. (36)

———

Jenny Holzer, Kara Walker, you know, their work is about activism. My work is maybe tangential to activism, but I think I am much more of a traditional painter in that sense. (36)

———

[I am not an activist-artist], not like Hank Willis Thomas, which is all activism. I just have a thread in everything. But I have another practice, 30% of my life is activism. (42)

———

I consider myself an artist who happens to be far left–leaning. And very concerned about it. I don't even think I'm that far left anymore. I used to be, but now I vote strategically. (25)

———

I was always for civil rights, and then anti-Vietnam. I worked for progressive politicians. I shut down the Pentagon. For reproductive rights, I went to Washington more than once … and I did all the marches. (6)

———

I read *Playboy* magazine. It was a really radical magazine for me in the Deep South. They had these great interviews and the pinups were not really that explicit. They were pro–reproduction rights, they were anti-Vietnam, they were pro–civil rights, they were really liberal in every way they could be, except for feminism just ripped their hearts out. (37)

I grew up fighting for civil rights down in the South and I just can't give it up. It's part of my DNA at this point. (20)

In the '80s there was a whole feminist movement trying to ban any kind of sexual imagery, pornography. That was the doctrinaire of feminism. It was a form of censorship from the left, which is so startling, especially being that I was such a feminist and such an activist. (34)

I believe you have to fight hate speech with good speech, not censorship. (6)

I was and continue to be anti-patriarchy, but I don't feel that I was too much woman. I just never tried to be a good girl or anything other than what I am. (18)

I'll always be an activist, though I am more of
a trickster propagandist than a moralist. (20)

———

I welcome change. I welcome a multicultural
country. I welcome when we're all a shade
of brown. (9)

———

I do work for Planned Parenthood, Downtown
for Democracy, Swing Left, among others.
The Trump cult we are fighting is strong. It's
the last gasp of a toxic patriarchy fighting for
a belief system that never worked. (20)

———

We are watching the last gasp of the patriarchy hanging on for dear life. (7)

———

Conservatives will continue to come for your civil rights—your birth control, your family planning, your ability to lead the kind of life you want and deserve. The violence and shattering of any sense of safety as a woman is not an unfortunate byproduct. It is the point. (50)

———

This toxic masculinity. Putin and his power grab for Ukraine—he's from another century. Everybody sees these images of him bombing women and children who are trying to leave through the humanitarian corridors, which are supposedly safe. That authoritarian male, that patriarchy that's ruling the world—it's poisonous. (19)

———

Celebrities have a hard time because the public grades them on a different curve. Artists have no problem, they're fearless. What are they going to do, not buy our work? Boycott? (13)

———

The women's movement, feminism,
I think is the biggest change I've seen in
my lifetime. (34)

———

Feminism makes sense, it's just rational.
Everyone is going to be better off. (45)

———

Being a feminist is really, I think, equal pay for
equal work and ownership of reproduction
over your own body. (35)

———

Planned Parenthood was available when I needed them in the '70s and they have been fighting for women's reproductive rights since they started. (3)

———

Feminism needs to include male feminists. It needs to include people of color. (13)

———

I think men are becoming proud to be called feminists and there is now inclusionary feminism. I think we have a new civil rights era. (45)

———

I think the opposite of a feminist is an asshole. That's how I look at it. I think you gotta be an asshole to be against feminism. (25)

———

I see entire civilizations based on policing women's bodies. I see it in our country with Republicans. (35)

———

The issues women face [today] are exactly the same but they have evolved. On the one hand, we're still fighting for equal pay for equal work, bodily autonomy, and reproductive rights. On the other, there are a lot more opportunities for women in all fields, and we have started to see a greater representation of women of color. (18)

———

It's so much better when you have parity.
I love what's happening with institutions
reaching for some balance. So many have been
marginalized for so long. And the BLM
movement now has a ton of allies.
That's what gets things to move. (25)

———

I'm not trying to be any kind of leader,
'cause it's not my generation. I don't need an
abortion, and I'm not going to get deported.
It's your generation. I just want to
be with you. (13)

———

Gen Z makes me hopeful. ... They are
the most justice-minded of any generation.
I mean, look at the kids who survived the
Parkland shooting. They're amazing.
My generation has to age out—we're
not going to change the baby
boomers' minds. (33)

———

I tell everybody: if they want to do anything,
join Swing Left. I do all kinds of things for
Swing Left. There really are things you can do!
Just be a volunteer. Because if you do *something*,
you'll feel a thousand times better.
I do it for myself. (25)

———

You get true, real joy out of helping someone, helping others, and fighting injustice. And I think if I didn't do it, I'd be going crazy right now. So it makes me feel I can make my work, I can compartmentalize somewhat, I can make my art, but if I wasn't an activist—I mean, if you're not upset right now, you're asleep. (37)

———

Silence is no longer an option. (54)

———

I don't really work with anybody who isn't a progressive political person. (4)

———

Do not give up hope. As Gloria Steinem—a self-proclaimed *hopeaholic*—regularly reminds us, it's vital that, despite it all, we act on our hopes every day. (50)

———

Move a muscle. Change a thought. (41)

———

Reflections on Art
and Life

The eye always craves what it doesn't see. (5)

———

The best art is always the simplest and most profound, and it's not art about art. (8)

———

Art's a language. It's an interpretation of our reality. It's a metaphor for what we're experiencing. It's satisfying because it creates a clear visual picture of some messy thoughts in that ocean of our brain. It makes something simple that's very complicated. (25)

———

I think there are as many ways to make art
as there are people making art. (26)

———

Art is meant to be nonlinear. It comes from
people's visions. (8)

———

I really believe this in my heart and soul, don't
be an artist unless you have no choice. It's just
too hard. It's constant rejection. (42)

———

There's not a piece of art made that you
can't find an argument against. (42)

———

It's corny, but … clichés are real. Sunsets are beautiful, and kittens are adorable! (56)

———

I don't try to make things happen anymore. I just make my work and hope the zeitgeist catches up to it. (10)

———

Most of the time, it's disappointing when your desires get met. That first bite of chocolate is heaven, but the second and third don't match up. (34)

———

Humanity is shot through with imperfection. We are really messy, untidy beings and trying to eliminate imperfection is making us sicker.

(7)

———

If you make rules, rules will spit in your face.

(53)

———

I am a Twitter junkie and I find Twitter to be sort of a rage machine, and I don't think it's really healthy for me. ... [R]ight now we are just pumped through to go where the rage is, right and left. We have to learn how to forgive each other. (2)

———

I travel all the time and I'm a museum aficionado. I love to look at art everywhere I go, but I think I'm a real American artist in the sense that I was brought up in a culture of imagery. A constant bombardment of advertising and imagery, and I think it probably molded the way I think. (12)

———

My work is in dialogue with and refers to the artistic practices of a lot of dead artists and all of art history. (52)

———

I go to museums and galleries all the time, but I can't see more than one floor of MoMA, otherwise I get brain overload. (52)

———

Artists are pretty delusional. They have to be. And they have to be totally self-involved and they have to be obsessive. (32)

———

Dear 2020, You've been a real bastard. I have blocked you on social media, deleted your number, and torn up your picture. Hope to never see you again, baby. It's not me, it's you. Fuck off, Marilyn Minter. (51)

———

Once you find your authentic voice, trust it.
(54)

———

Life is so complicated. I like to try and mimic
that in my art. (26)

———

I really believe that if you are going to be an
artist, it's not like you have a choice, you just
are. Whether you like it or not, you have
to do it. I believe that it's so much
easier not to be one. (31)

———

After I learned about Warhol and Pop Art
I found my comfort zone. (12)

———

Being marginalized keeps you hungry.
That's my theory, anyway. (1)

Most of the people I know who have any
talent come from a lot of pain. (31)

If you listen to your inner vision and listen to
your own voice, and make art from that place,
sooner or later the zeitgeist hits you. (5)

Multiple meanings, multiple reads. That's all
I'm interested in—metaphor and paradox. (45)

I want you to come with your own history and your own traditions to have a dialogue with the work. (55)

———

It could be that art history is predicated on critique. You have to find something wrong with everybody, and that's how you make your name. I'm always questioning that. (8)

———

Envy is a killer. It's the most wasteful energy. (29)

———

If you have integrity in your work, that shines through. This is my first retrospective [at the Brooklyn Museum in 2016], and I'm 68. Yeah, it's my first one, fuck you. I'm not going anywhere. (21)

———

When you have a certain amount of money, you're expected to erase the aging process. And if you don't do it, there's something wrong with you. (19)

———

There wasn't even any acknowledgment of trans people 10 years ago. Now "gay" is part of the vernacular. (8)

———

I don't try to make things happen. They're either going to flow, or I leave them alone. (47)

———

I did a massive amount of drugs to be able to loosen up. That's not really what my gift is. … It's only since I cleaned up my act that I could start to focus on what I was good at, and then I started believing in my inner voice. (4)

———

I feel like I have made the same image over and over and over, they just look different— from the time I was 12. Honestly, I feel like … they are all the same and I just want to grow and change and become a better artist. I feel like … I haven't made it yet. (2)

———

The academy never saw Warhol. They never saw Haring. They never saw anything that was accepted by popular culture. It's embarrassing! Matisse didn't sell a painting in France until he was old! (8)

———

Most art has to fail before it succeeds. (54)

———

I love to work. I have so much pleasure making work. (20)

———

I don't ever want to tell anyone what to think. Come to your own conclusions. You're going to do it anyway. (4)

———

SOURCES

The quotes included in this publication have been lightly edited by
  the author.

1. Stead, Chloe. "Marilyn Minter on Overcoming Censor-
    ship and Bringing Back Pubic Hair." *Frieze*, July 21, 2021.
    https://www.frieze.com/article/marilyn-minter-all-wet
    -interview.
2. Aton, Francesca. "Artist Marilyn Minter on Depicting the
    Unexpected and Reclaiming Images of Women." Interview
    by Brooke Jaffe. *Artnews*, April 30, 2021. https://www
    .artnews.com/art-news/artists/marilyn-minter-artnews
    -live-interview-1234591349/.
3. "Interview with Marilyn Minter." Interview by *Her Clique*.
    https://herclique.com/blogs/stories/interview-with
    -marilyn-minter.
4. Siemsen, Thora. "On Listening to Your Inner Voice."
    Creative Independent, November 13, 2018. https:
    //thecreativeindependent.com/people/visual-artist
    -marilyn-minter-on-listening-to-your-inner-voice/.
5. Artspace Editors. "Marilyn Minter on Art, Life &
    Everything In Between." *Artspace*, August 30, 2022. https:
    //www.artspace.com/magazine/interviews_features

/need-to-know/marilyn-minter-on-art-life-everything
-in-between-57160.

6. Grillo. "The Lenny Interview: Marilyn Minter." *Lenny*,
    March 30, 2018. https://www.lennyletter.com/story/the
    -lenny-interview-marilyn-minter.

7. Kordic, Angie. "Beauty, Desire, Pleasure, Feminism—In
    Conversation with Marilyn Minter." *Widewalls*, April 14,
    2021. https://www.widewalls.ch/magazine/marilyn
    -minter-podcast.

8. Simmons, William J. "Marilyn Minter Works in the
    Gray Area." *Standard Hotels*, March 8, 2017. https://www
    .standardhotels.com/culture/marilyn-minter-interview.

9. Funk, Mia. "Photographer Marilyn Minter Interviewed by
    Mia Funk." *Creative Process*. https://www.creativeprocess.
    info/interviews-9/marilyn-minter-mia-funk.

10. Ekstrand, Anna Mikaela. "Laurie Simmons and Marilyn
    Minter Talk Motherhood, Envy, and Inspiration." *Cultbytes*,
    July 13, 2022. https://cultbytes.com/laurie-simmons
    -and-marilyn-minter-talk-motherhood-envy-and
    -inspiration/.

11. Mason, Petra. "Interview with Artist Marilyn Minter
    and Curator Ariella Wolens: Part 1." *Whitehot Magazine*, July
    2020. https://whitehotmagazine.com/articles/curator
    -ariella-wolens-part-1/4655.

12. Honoré, Vincent. "Marilyn Minter: In Conversation

with Vincent Honoré." *Cura.*32, October issue. https:
//curamagazine.com/digital/marilyn-minter/.

13. Worthman, Jenna. "Marilyn Minter Finds Art in the Female
    Form." *New York Times*, February 15, 2017. https://www
    .nytimes.com/2017/02/15/magazine/marilyn-minter
    -finds-art-in-the-female-form.html.

14. Kovler, Anna. "Interview: Marilyn Minter and Jasmine
    Wahi." *Arsenal Contemporary*, January 2020. https://www
    .arsenalcontemporary.com/press/2020/01/interview
    -marilyn-minter-and-jasmine-wahi.

15. Eric Minh Swenson Art Films. "Marilyn Minter: Pretty/
    Dirty." YouTube, June 16, 2016. https://www.youtube
    .com/watch?v=qMNGNn6CdwY&t=2s.

16. Creative Time. "Interview with Marilyn Minter." YouTube,
    November 4, 2009. https://www.youtube.com
    /watch?v=l5Ujh9iOThE.

17. Blouin Artinfo. "AI Interview Marilyn Minter at Salon
    94 Bowery." YouTube, December 9, 2011. https://www
    .youtube.com/watch?v=hmE-ygycjWU.

18. Flora, Rachael. "deFINE ART: A Conversation with Marilyn
    Minter." *Connect Savannah*, February 19, 2020. https:
    //www.connectsavannah.com/savannah/a-conversation
    -with-marilyn-minter/Content?oid=14063917.

19. "Legendary Noncomformists Marilyn Minter and Michele
    Lamy on Sex, Aging, and Beauty." *Harper's Bazaar*, May 11,

2022. https://www.harpersbazaar.com/culture/art-books
-music/a39697807/in-conversation-marilyn-minter-and
-michele-lamy-may-2022/.

20. "Episode 26 Marilyn Minter." *Lydian Spin*, January 11, 2020.
https://lydianspin.libsyn.com/episode-26-marilyn-minter.

21. Iversen, Kristin. "Drinking Seltzer and Getting Life Advice
from Marilyn Minter." *Nylon*, 2016. https://www.nylon
.com/articles/marilyn-minter-interview.

22. McCormick, Carlo. "Marilyn Minter: The Constant Rebel."
Juxtapoz, 2020. https://www.juxtapoz.com/news
/magazine/features/marilyn-minter-a-constant-rebel/.

23. Green, Tyler. "Summer Clips: Marilyn Minter." *Modern Art
Notes Podcast*, 2023. https://soundcloud.com/manpodcast
/ep552.

24. Myers, Marc. "Artist Marilyn Minter Turned to the Brush
and Camera to Escape Childhood Woes." *Wall Street Journal*,
March 8, 2022. https://www.wsj.com/articles/painter
-marilyn-minter-turned-to-the-brush-and-camera-to
-escape-childhood-woes-11646755113.

25. Feinstein, Laura. "Marilyn Minter Wants You to Vote."
Slow Ghost, November 1, 2020. https://slowghost.substack
.com/p/marilyn-minter-wants-you-to-vote.

26. Goldstein, Richard. "Marilyn Minter at the Strand." *Bomb*
magazine, June 21, 2010. https://bombmagazine.org
/articles/marilyn-minter/.

27. Davies, Bree. "Marilyn Minter Talks Photoshop, Feminism, Fashion and Fine Art." *Westword*, September 16, 2015. https://www.westword.com/arts/marilyn-minter-talks-photoshop-feminism-fashion-and-fine-art-7148588.

28. Regensdorf, Laura. "Artist Marilyn Minter Talks Beauty Norms, the Return of the Full Bush, and Her New Retrospective." *Vogue*, November 4, 2016. https://www.vogue.com/article/marilyn-minter-pretty-dirty-retrospective-brooklyn-museum-body-hair-beauty-norms-feminism.

29. Munro, Cait. "Marilyn Minter on Glamour, Diane Arbus, and Why Envy Is the Worst Emotion." *Artnet*, September 17, 2015. https://news.artnet.com/art-world/marilyn-minter-interview-330297.

30. "Marilyn Minter." *Brooklyn Rail*, March 2015. https://brooklynrail.org/2015/03/criticspage/marilyn-minter-mar15.

31. "Public Program Archive: Marilyn Minter Artist Talk." SFMOMA, April 21, 2005. https://soundcloud.com/sfmoma/public-programs-archive-1.

32. Holmes, Helen. "Marilyn Minter Changed Art. She Is Still 'Filthy' and Fabulous." *Daily Beast*, December 24, 2022. https://www.thedailybeast.com/marilyn-minter-changed-art-she-is-still-filthy-and-fabulous.

33. Giles, Oliver. "Artist Marilyn Minter: 'Donald Trump Is a

Monster.' " *Tatler*, October 3, 2018. https://www.tatlerasia
.com/lifestyle/arts/hk-marilyn-minter-donald-trump.

34. Wallin, Yasha. "Marilyn Minter: The Pain and Pleasure of
Desire." *Edition*. https://theeditionbroadsheet.com/article
/marilyn-minter/.

35. Vartanian, Hrag. "Marilyn Minter and Xaviera Simmons Talk
Art, Sex, and Democracy." *Hyperallergic*, December 22, 2016.
https://hyperallergic.com/347099/marilyn-minter-and
-xaviera-simmons-talk-art-sex-and-democracy/.

36. "Marilyn Minter. All Wet." *Mo.Co.*, 2021. https://www
.moco.art/en/exposition/marilyn-minter-all-wet.

37. Millman, Debbie. "Design Matters from the Archive:
Marilyn Minter." *Print*, February 15, 2021. https://www
.printmag.com/podcasts/2021/design-matters-from-the
-archive%3A-marilyn-minter/.

38. Fletcher, Gem. "The Beauty Paradox: In Conversation
with Marilyn Minter." *September Issues*, May 2, 2020. https
://www.theseptemberissues.com/the-beauty-paradox/.

39. Daniel, Daria. "*Artnet* Asks: Marilyn Minter Calls Herself
a Photo-Replacer." *Artnet*, April 12, 2015. https://news
.artnet.com/art-world/artnet-asks-marilyn-minter-285520.

40. "Artist Marilyn Minter on Styling Pubic Hair & Depicting
Female Sexuality." *VICE Life*, September 30, 2015. https:
//www.youtube.com/watch?v=voLHQWJS4-M.

41. "Marilyn Minter—Hirshhorn Artist Diaries." *Hirshhorn*,

April 27, 2020. https://www.youtube.com/watch?v=g
-Tvd2gSaSE.

42. "Marilyn Minter—Fine Artist." School of Visual Arts,
November 20, 2019. https://www.youtube.com
/watch?v=h2YfSyMsA5M.

43. Holmes, Helen. "Marilyn Minter Talks Gaga, Gay Talese
Talks Juul at MoMA's 'The Price of Everything' After-Party."
Observer, October 23, 2018. https://observer.com/2018
/10/marilyn-minter-talks-gaga-gay-talese-talks-juul
-momas-the-price-of-everything-after-party/.

44. O'Brien, Glenn. "Marilyn Minter." *Purple*, 2013. https:
//purple.fr/magazine/ss-2013-issue-19/marilyn-minter/.

45. "Brooklyn Talks: Madonna X Marilyn Minter [January 19,
2017]." *Madonna Vault Videos*, March 9, 2017. https://www
.youtube.com/watch?v=DfRRZU73ygY.

46. Yablonsky, Linda. "Beauty in the Details: Marilyn Minter
in Conversation with Linda Yablonsky." In *Marilyn Minter
Pretty/Dirty*, 35–39. New York: Gregory R. Miller, 2015.

47. Schwiegershausen, Erica. "How I Get It Done: Artist
Marilyn Minter." *The Cut*, September 30, 2019. https:
//www.thecut.com/2019/09/how-i-get-it-done-artist
-marilyn-minter.html.

48. Gerard, Sarah. "Marilyn on Top: Artist and Floridian
Marilyn Minter Opens Up." *Flamingo*, September 7, 2019.
https://flamingomag.com/2019/09/07/marilyn-minter/.

49. "'The Culture Will Never Go Back': A Q&A with Artist and 2021 SVA Commencement Speaker Marilyn Minter." School of Visual Arts, May 5, 2021. https://sva.edu /features/the-culture-will-never-go-back-a-q-and-a -with-artist-and-2021-sva-commencement-speaker -marilyn-minter.

50. Minter, Marilyn. "Artist and Activist Marilyn Minter on Roe Leak: This Is 'What Minority Rule Looks Like.'" Artnews, May 5, 2022. https://www.artnews.com/art-news/news /artist-and-activist-marilyn-minter-on-roe-wade-supreme -court-leak-1234627748/.

51. Regensdorf, Laura. "Marilyn Minter, Joy Harjo, and More Give a Colorful Kiss-Off to 2020." Vanity Fair, December 18, 2020. https://www.vanityfair.com/style/2020/12 /lipstick-kiss-off-2020.

52. McDermott, Emily. "My First Art Basel: Marilyn Minter." Paris+ par Art Basel. https://parisplus.artbasel.com /news/50-years-my-first-art-basel-marilyn-minter.

53. Mason, Petra. "Nasty Women: Marilyn Minter Interview Part 2." Whitehot Magazine, 2020. https://whitehotmagazine .com/articles/marilyn-minter-interview-part-2/4672.

54. Perez, Rodrigo. "Discover Your 'Authentic Voice': 2021 SVA Commencement Highlights and Marilyn Minter's Keynote Speech." School of Visual Arts, May 23, 2021. https://sva .edu/features/discover-your-authentic-voice-2021-sva -commencement-highlights-and-marilyn-minter-s-key

note-speech.

55. "Artist Talk: Marilyn Minter." Princeton University Art Museum, June 23, 2022. https://artmuseum.princeton .edu/false/video/learn/artist-talk-marilyn-minter.

56. Miller, Steve. "Established Artist: Marilyn Minter; Glamour-puss." *Musee*, July 1, 2014. https://www.regenprojects .com/attachment/en/54522d19cfaf3430698b4568 /Press/5b00c19ba7d750ca7a7fdfb0.

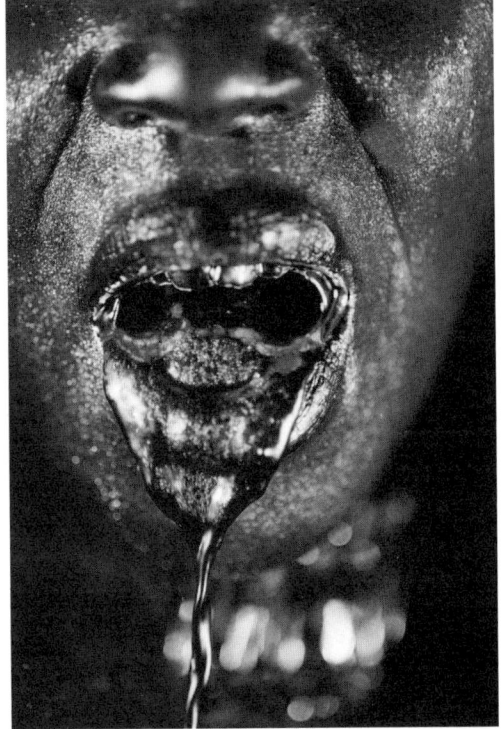

CHRONOLOGY

1948

Marilyn Minter is born in Shreveport, Louisiana, on July 20. She is raised by her parents, whom she describes as a "pill-popping drug addict" (her mother) and "an alcoholic, compulsive gambler, and womanizer" (her father).

1956

Minter's parents split.

1964

At sixteen, Minter is arrested and jailed for one night for altering a driver's license to get into bars.

1969

While in college, Minter photographs her mother at home in Fort Lauderdale, Florida, during a weekend visit. She creates a series of intimate black-and-white photographs that reflect the reality of her mother's life with addiction.

1970

Minter receives her BFA from the University of Florida, Gainesville.

1972

Minter receives her MFA in painting from Syracuse University, Syracuse, New York.

1975

Minter's first solo exhibition opens at the Everson Museum of Art in Syracuse.

1976

Minter moves to New York City with her first husband, George Harris. They divorce and she begins collaborating with German Expressionist artist Christof Kohlhofer. Minter also works as an assistant to sculptor Kenneth Snelson and teaches evening art classes to retirees in Brooklyn.

1979

Minter uses the bathroom in her apartment as a dark-
   room to produce photographs. She begins a series
   of photorealist paintings based on her photos.

1983

Minter's mother dies.

1984

Minter and Kohlhofer exhibit their work at Gracie
   Mansion Gallery on Manhattan's Lower East Side.

1986

Minter breaks off the collaboration with Kohlhofer.

1988

Minter receives an artist's fellowship from the New York
   Foundation for the Arts.

1989

Minter has solo exhibitions at Nicola Jacobs Gallery
in London and White Columns in New York City.
She receives a Visual Arts Fellowship grant from the
National Endowment for the Arts. She begins her
exploration of pornography and art with the *Food
Porn* series. Minter also creates *Porn Grid*, a series of
four-panel paintings of graphic sexual scenes sourced
from a pornography magazine. The work is savaged
by critics and she is called a "traitor to feminism"
for her pro-sex feminist stance.

1990

Minter has solo shows at the Max Protetch and Simon
Watson galleries in New York City. She produces
her first video, *100 Food Porn*, shot and directed by
documentary filmmaker Ted Haimes, to promote
her exhibition at the Simon Watson gallery. Using
the advertising budget intended for traditional print
advertising, she instead purchases thirty-second slots
on *Late Night with David Letterman*, *Arsenio Hall*, and
Nightline, becoming the first artist to advertise an

exhibition on late-night television. Minter is represented in group exhibitions at Simon Watson Gallery, Fiction/Nonfiction Gallery, and Andrea Rosen Gallery, all in New York City.

1991

Minter has solo exhibitions at Greenberg Gallery in Saint Louis, Missouri, and Meyers/Bloom Gallery in Santa Monica, California. She is represented in group exhibitions at John Post Lee Gallery, New York City, and Carnegie Mellon Art Gallery, Pittsburgh.

1992

Minter has solo exhibitions at John C. Stoller & Co., Minneapolis, and Max Protetch Gallery in New York City, where she exhibits her porn paintings for the first time. She receives an Artists' Fellowship Visual Arts grant from the New York Foundation for the Arts. She is represented in group exhibitions at the Carnegie Museum of Art, Pittsburgh; PS1 Contemporary Art Center, New York City; and Galerie 1900–2000, Paris.

1993

Minter participates in group exhibitions at White Columns, David Zwirner, and the DIA Center for the Arts (all in New York City); at the Arthur Roger Gallery, New Orleans; and TRI Gallery, Los Angeles.

1994

Minter is represented in group exhibitions at the Inter Art Center, Adam Baumgold Fine Art, the Kitchen, Trial Balloon, and Max Protetch Gallery (all in New York City); the Cummings Art Center at Connecticut College, New London; and the Sprengel Museum, Hannover, Germany.

1995

Writer and curator Linda Yablonsky organizes an evening of readings at the Drawing Center in New York City. She includes a selection of the black-and-white photographs that Minter took of her mother in 1969. The event revitalizes her career. Minter has solo exhibitions at Max Protetch and Postmasters galleries in

New York City and at TRI Gallery in Los Angeles. She
participates in group exhibitions at Neue Galerie and
Landesmuseum Joanneum and Künstlerhaus in Graz,
Austria; and Roger Merians Gallery and Here Gallery,
both in New York City.

1996
Minter is represented in several group exhibitions,
including *Thinking Print: Books to Billboards, 1980–1995*
at the Museum of Modern Art, New York City, among
several others.

1997
Minter has a solo exhibition at XL Xavier LaBoulbenne
and is represented in group exhibitions at Elizabeth
Harris Gallery and Stefan Stux Gallery (all in New
York City).

1998
Minter is featured in solo exhibitions at Index in Stockholm and XL Xavier LaBoulbenne, New York City, and

participates in a group exhibition at the Museum of Fine Arts, Boston, among several others. She receives a Guggenheim fellowship from the John Simon Guggenheim Memorial Foundation.

1999

Minter is represented in group exhibitions at Exit Art, New York City; Bard College, Annandale-on-Hudson, New York; and Arcadia University Art Gallery, Glenside, Pennsylvania.

2000

Minter has solo exhibitions at Andréhn-Schiptjenko in Stockholm and XL Xavier LaBoulbenne in New York City. She participates in group exhibitions at Galería Leyendecker, Santa Cruz de Tenerife in the Canary Islands, Spain; Galerie Thaddaeus Ropac, Paris; and Gimpel Fils, London, among others.

2001

Minter has a solo exhibition at Galerie Thaddaeus Ropac,

Paris, and is represented in a group exhibition at Sandroni.Rey in Venice, California. She marries her second husband, Bill Miller.

2002
Minter participates in group exhibitions at Exit Art, New York City, and Arnolfini in Bristol, England (traveling to Cornerhouse in Manchester, England).

2003
Minter has a solo exhibition at Fredericks & Freiser, New York City. She is represented in group exhibitions at Arena Gallery, Cheim & Read, and Gorney Bravin + Lee Gallery (all in New York City) and Henry Art Gallery in Seattle, Washington.

2004
Minter is featured in solo exhibitions at Andréhn-Schiptjenko in Stockholm and Baldwin Gallery in Aspen, Colorado, and in group exhibitions at Regen Projects, Los Angeles; Greenberg Van Doren Gallery, New York City; and Union Station, Toronto, Canada.

2005

New Work: Marilyn Minter is presented at the San Francisco
Museum of Modern Art. She has a solo exhibition at
Voges + Partner, Frankfurt, Germany. Minter receives
the Biennial Award from the Louis Comfort Tiffany
Foundation. She is represented in group exhibitions
at HangarBicocca, Milan, Italy, and Patricia Faure Gallery, Santa Monica, California, among several others.

2006

Minter's work is featured in the Whitney Biennial.
The first monograph of her work is published. In
a partnership with Creative Time in New York City,
she is given a month of space on four billboards in
Manhattan's Chelsea district. Minter has her first solo
exhibition with Salon 94, New York City. She also has
solo exhibitions at Baldwin Gallery, Aspen, Colorado;
Circuit in Lausanne, Switzerland; and Gavlak Projects,
Palm Beach, Florida. Minter is also represented in
group exhibitions at Spanierman Modern, Marvelli
Gallery, and Tony Shafrazi Gallery (all in New York
City).

2007

Minter produces a series of photographs of the actress
Pamela Anderson, commissioned by the quarterly
art magazine *Parkett*. Minter is represented in group
exhibitions at the Chelsea Art Museum, New York
City (traveling to Naples, Italy); Norrköpings Konst-
museum, Norrköpings, Sweden; DUMBO Arts Center,
Brooklyn; and the Tacoma Art Museum, Tacoma,
Washington, among others.

2008

Minter is featured in a solo exhibition at Andréhn-
Schiptjenko in Stockholm. She collaborates with
skate and streetwear brand Supreme to produce
three limited-edition skate decks and participates
in group exhibitions at Fotomuseum in Winterthur,
Switzerland; the Busan Biennale in Busan, Korea;
and the Denver Art Museum, Denver, Colorado,
among others.

2009

Minter presents four solo exhibitions, including *Chewing*

Color at the Contemporary Arts Center, Cincinnati, Ohio; and *Green Pink Caviar* at Salon 94 Freemans, New York City; La Conservera, Centro de Arte Contemporáneo in Ceutí, Spain; and Regen Projects, Los Angeles. Minter is represented in group exhibitions at 21st Century Museum of Contemporary Art in Kanazawa, Japan; Cheim & Read, New York City; De Markten in Brussels, Belgium; Lehmann Maupin, New York City; and SITE Santa Fe in Santa Fe, New Mexico, among others. She participates in the Conversations program at Art Basel Miami Beach in Miami, Florida.

2009–10

Minter is commissioned by Creative Time to create her video work *Green Pink Caviar*. The piece is broadcast for the first time on MTV's digital billboard in New York City's Times Square. Excerpts of the video are used as the backdrop for the opening song in Madonna's "Sticky and Sweet" tour.

2010

Minter is featured in the solo exhibitions *Orange Crush* at the Museum of Contemporary Art Cleveland and *Green Pink Caviar* at the Museum of Modern Art in New York City. She is also represented in group exhibitions at the San Francisco Museum of Modern Art and the Baltimore Museum of Art, Baltimore, Maryland, among others.

2011

Minter is in three solo exhibitions: *Paintings from the 80s* at Team Gallery, New York City; *Marilyn Minter*, a retrospective at Deichtorhallen in Hamburg, Germany; and *Marilyn Minter* at Salon 94 Bowery, New York City. She also participates in group exhibitions at the Garage Center for Contemporary Culture in Moscow and the Venice Bienniale.

2012

Minter is featured in the group exhibition *Riotous Baroque*. Originating at the Kunsthaus Zürich in Switzerland, it later travels to the Guggenheim Bilbao. She also participates in group exhibitions at the Louisiana Museum of Modern Art in Humlebæk, Denmark, and the Robert Rauschenberg Foundation Project Space in New York City, among others.

2013

Minter has a solo exhibition at Regen Projects, Los Angeles. She is represented in group exhibitions at White Columns in New York City and Schirn Kunsthalle in Frankfurt, Germany, among others.

2014

Minter publishes *Plush*, a limited-edition book featuring seventy photographs of female pubic hair, with Richard Prince's publishing company, Fulton Ryder. *Playboy* commissions Minter for a special edition of the magazine intended to feature artist-conceived photo spreads. Minter's proposed contribution, *Bring Back the Bush*, is a series of close-up photographs of female pubic hair adorned with flowers, pearls, and gold chains. Ultimately *Playboy* rejects the photos and substitutes a small detail of one of the images. Minter participates in several group shows, including locations such as the San Francisco Museum of Modern Art and the Brooklyn Museum, among many other prominent museums and galleries.

2015

Minter's retrospective *Marilyn Minter: Pretty/Dirty* opens at the Contemporary Arts Museum Houston and later travels to the Museum of Contemporary Art in Denver. Group exhibitions at the Rose Art Museum, Brandeis University, Waltham, Massachusetts; White Columns, New York City; Kyiv Biennial, Ukraine; and David Roberts Art Foundation, London, among others.

2016

Marilyn Minter: Pretty/Dirty travels to the Orange County Museum of Art in Newport Beach, California. Minter presents a solo show at Salon 94, New York City, and is in group exhibitions at the Museum of Contemporary Art Cleveland (moCa); Museumsfreunde Weserburg, Bremen, Germany; and Maccarone Gallery, New York City, among others.

2016–17
Marilyn Minter: Pretty/Dirty is presented at the Brooklyn Museum.

2018
Minter is featured in solo exhibitions at Lehmann Maupin in Hong Kong and Regen Projects in Los Angeles. She collaborates with For Freedoms—an artist-run platform for civic engagement—to create a billboard poster for the 50 State Initiative, a major billboard campaign that encourages political participation and voting. Displayed in Little Rock, Arkansas, Minter's billboard resembles graffiti, with the word "sad!" in red, blue, and purple spray paint. Minter intended for her billboard to criticize Donald Trump, stating, "I would have been really aggressive if I could. ... This is as mild as I could get."

She also participates in group exhibitions at the Louisiana Museum of Modern Art in Humlebæk, Denmark; San Francisco Museum of Modern Art; and Ryan Lee Gallery, New York City.

2019
Minter's exhibition at Simon Lee Gallery in London is her first solo presentation in the UK in thirty years. She is among three awardees for the 3rd Annual Badass Art Woman Awards presented by Project for Empty Space. The fall issue of *Playboy*, dedicated to pleasure, features Minter's work. She is also featured in group exhibitions at the Museum of Fine Arts, Boston, and Spring Studios, New York City, among several others.

2020
Minter is an honoree and keynote speaker at the 11th annual edition of the Savannah College of Art and Design's deFINE ART program of exhibitions, lectures, and performances. Her solo exhibition

Nasty Woman is featured at the SCAD Museum of Art. Minter is represented in group exhibitions at Copenhagen Contemporary in Denmark and Jeffrey Deitch, Los Angeles, among many others.

2021

Minter's solo exhibitions include *Smash* at the Museum of Contemporary Art Westport (MoCA CT), Westport, Connecticut; *Marilyn Minter* at Lehmann Maupin, Beijing; and *All Wet* at MO.CO., Montpellier, France. As a longtime faculty member of the School of Visual Arts MFA Fine Arts program, she gives the keynote address at SVA's 46th annual commencement exercises. Due to the Covid pandemic, the event takes place online.

2022

Minter's work is included in *Women Painting Women* at the Modern Art Museum of Fort Worth, Texas.

2023

Marilyn Minter: Elder Sex is published by JBE Books, Paris, and LGDR, New York City. Minter's solo show at LGDR features paintings of American singers Lady Gaga and Lizzo.

2024

Minter is featured in a solo exhibition at Lehmann Maupin in Seoul, Korea, and participates in group exhibitions at Regen Projects and Anat Ebgi in Los Angeles, California.

ACKNOWLEDGMENTS

First, I would like to express my heartfelt thanks to Marilyn Minter, whose dedication to pushing the boundaries of art is an inspiration to us all. It is an honor to bring your profound insights and empowering words to these pages.

My thanks as well to Marianna Peragallo, Michelle Girardello, Genevieve Lowe, Liz Dragan, and the entire studio team for crucial assistance in the research process.

My sincere appreciation, as always, to the entire team at Princeton University Press, especially Michelle Komie, Christie Henry, Terri O'Prey, Cathy Slovensky, Jacqueline Poirier, Colleen Suljic, Laurie Schlesinger, Cathy Felgar, Jodi Price, Kathryn Stevens, Annie Miller, William Skurka, and Alexandria Leonard. We remain extremely grateful to PUP for their continued professionalism, encouragement, and passion for our projects together throughout the years.

I would also like to extend my profound thanks to Louise Donegan, whose wisdom, guidance, and support have been instrumental in shaping my understanding and approach to feminist issues, and whose friendship I continue to value greatly.

My thanks and admiration to Jeanne Greenberg Rohatyn as well, who has been a steadfast champion of Marilyn's work over the years.

Very special thanks to Taliesin Thomas for her invaluable research for this project, and to Fiona Graham for her excellent organization of the ISMs series as a whole. My thanks as well to Susan Delson for her essential editorial insights.

My sincere thanks to Karen Lautanen for her organizational aid on this project and many others, and to Steven Rodríguez for his continued support.

Finally, I give all my bottomless gratitude to my amazing wife, Abbey, and to my wonderful children, Justin, Ethan, Ellie, and Jonah for their love and encouragement.

As always, I give endless love and thanks to my mother Judith.

LARRY WARSH

Marilyn Minter (born 1948) is an American artist currently living and working in New York City. Minter's work has been the subject of numerous solo exhibitions and has been included in group exhibitions in museums all over the world. In 2006, Minter was included in the Whitney Biennial and installed several billboards in Chelsea, New York City, in collaboration with Creative Time. Her video *Green Pink Caviar* was exhibited in the lobby of the MoMA from 2010–11. It was also shown on digital billboards on Sunset Boulevard in Los Angeles and on the Creative Time MTV billboard in Times Square, New York. In 2013, Minter was featured in *Riotous Baroque*, an exhibition that originated at the Kunsthaus Zürich and traveled to the Guggenheim Bilbao. In 2015, Minter's retrospective *Pretty/Dirty* opened at the Contemporary Arts Museum in Houston, Texas. *Pretty/Dirty* traveled to the Museum of Contemporary Art, Denver; the Orange County Museum of Art; and the Brooklyn Museum in November 2016. Minter is represented by Salon 94, New York; Regen Projects, Los Angeles; Lehmann Maupin, Seoul; and Baldwin Gallery, Aspen.

Minter is the recipient of numerous prestigious awards, including the Guggenheim Fellowship (1998) and the Louis Comfort Tiffany Grant (2006). Her work is in the collections of many museums globally, including the MIT List Center, Cambridge (MA); the Museum of Contemporary Art, Los Angeles (CA); the Museum of Fine Arts, Boston (MA); the Museum of Modern Art, New York (NY); the Perez Art Museum, Miami (FL); the Tate Modern, London (UK); the Solomon R. Guggenheim Museum, New York (NY); and the Whitney Museum of American Art, New York (NY), among many others.

Larry Warsh has been active in the art world for more than thirty years as a publisher and artist-collaborator. An early collector of Keith Haring and Jean-Michel Basquiat, Warsh was a lead organizer for the exhibition *Basquiat: The Unknown Notebooks*, which debuted at the Brooklyn Museum, New York, in 2015, and later traveled to several American museums. He has loaned artworks by Haring and Basquiat from his collection to numerous exhibitions worldwide, and he served as a curatorial consultant on *Keith Haring | Jean-Michel Basquiat: Crossing Lines* for the National Gallery of Victoria. The founder of *Museums Magazine*, Warsh has been involved in many publishing projects and is the editor of the ISMs series and several other titles published by Princeton University Press, including Jean-Michel Basquiat's *The Notebooks* (2017), *Keith Haring: 31 Subway Drawings* (2021), and two books by Ai Weiwei, *Humanity* (2018) and *Weiwei-isms* (2012). Warsh has served on the board of the Getty Museum Photographs Council and was a founding member of the Basquiat Authentication Committee until its dissolution in 2012.

ILLUSTRATIONS

Frontispiece: Portrait of Marilyn Minter. Photograph
© Ryan McGinley.

Page 108: Marilyn Minter, *Wangechi Gold #5*, 2009.
Dye sublimation print. Courtesy of the artist, Salon 94,
New York, and Regen Projects, Los Angeles.

ISMs

Larry Warsh, Series Editor

The ISMs series distills the voices of an exciting range of visual artists and designers into captivating, beautifully made books of quotations for a new generation of readers. In turn passionate, inspiring, humorous, witty, and challenging, these collections offer powerful statements on topics ranging from contemporary culture, politics, and race, to creativity, humanity, and the role of art in the world. Books in this series are edited by Larry Warsh and published by Princeton University Press in association with No More Rulers.